The Moon

Michael Jay

Franklin Watts
London New York Toronto Sydney

© 1982 Franklin Watts Ltd

First published in Great Britain in
    1982 by
Franklin Watts Ltd
8 Cork Street
London W1

First published in the USA by
Franklin Watts Inc.
730 Fifth Avenue
New York
N.Y. 10019

UK edition: 0 85166 954 9
US edition: 0-531-04373-8
Library of Congress Catalog Card
    Number: 81-70051

Printed in Great Britain by E. T.
    Heron, London and Essex

Photographs supplied by
NASA
Space Frontiers Ltd

Illustrated by
Christopher Forsey
Product Support Graphics
Michael Roffe

Designed and produced by
David Jefferis

Technical consultants
Nigel Henbest MSc, FRAS
Iain Nicholson BSc, FRAS

AN
EASY-READ
FACT
BOOK

The Moon

Contents

Birth of the Moon

The Moon is planet Earth's natural satellite, the world's neighbor in space. It circles the Earth at a distance of nearly 239,000 miles (384,000 km).

Scientists think that five billion years ago, the Moon was nothing but a tiny part of a vast swirling cloud of dust and gases. The material in the middle of the cloud eventually formed the Sun. The rest formed the planets, including the Earth and its satellite, the Moon.

The young Moon was hit by millions of chunks of rock. These meteorites were the material remaining in space after the Sun and planets were formed. They scarred the Moon's surface with craters.

The last big meteorite shower took place about three billion years ago. Since then, the Moon has changed little, as it has no wind or weather to wear away and change its features.

▷ Nearly five billion years ago, Earth and Moon could have looked like this – two balls of dust and gas, gradually sweeping up fragments of matter as they slowly circle in space. By examining moonrocks, scientists have been able to date the "birth" of the Moon 4.6 billion years ago.

Earth and Moon compared

The Moon is Earth's nearest neighbor, but the two worlds are very different. The Earth has a blanket of air and most of it is covered with water. It is teeming with life. The Moon has no air, no water and is completely lifeless.

An Earth day is 24 hours long. The Moon turns very slowly on its axis, so its "days" are much longer – they last almost as long as a month on Earth.

The Moon is smaller than the Earth. Its pull of gravity is less. Things weigh only one-sixth as much on the Moon as they do on Earth.

▽ If Earth were the size shown below, the Moon would be about 12 in (30 cm) away. They are really 238,867 miles (384,401 km) apart.

▷ Earth is 7,927 miles (12,756 km) across. The Moon is much smaller. Its diameter is about one quarter the size, 2,160 miles (3,476 km).

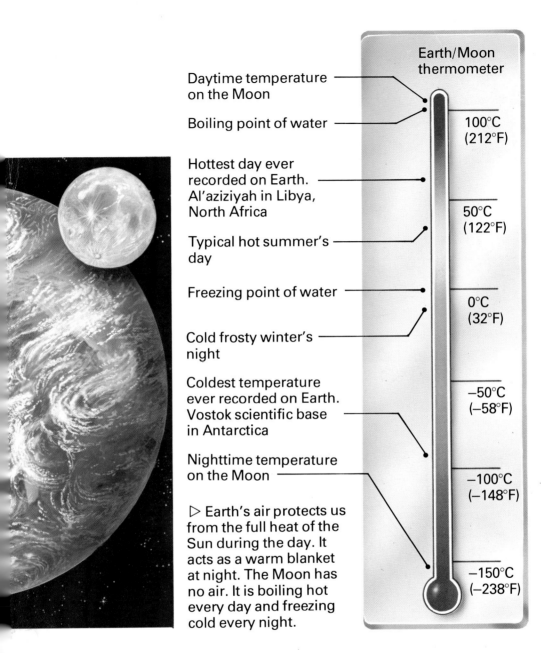

Daytime temperature on the Moon

Boiling point of water

Hottest day ever recorded on Earth. Al'aziziyah in Libya, North Africa

Typical hot summer's day

Freezing point of water

Cold frosty winter's night

Coldest temperature ever recorded on Earth. Vostok scientific base in Antarctica

Nighttime temperature on the Moon

Earth/Moon thermometer

100°C (212°F)

50°C (122°F)

0°C (32°F)

−50°C (−58°F)

−100°C (−148°F)

−150°C (−238°F)

▷ Earth's air protects us from the full heat of the Sun during the day. It acts as a warm blanket at night. The Moon has no air. It is boiling hot every day and freezing cold every night.

7

Phases of the Moon

The full Moon is the brightest object we can see in the night sky. It does not glow like the Sun. Its light is reflected sunshine.

As the Moon orbits the Earth, different amounts of its sunlit side can be seen. This changing shape is called the phase. The Moon circles the Earth once every $27\frac{1}{3}$ days, so each phase occurs every month.

△ The pictures above show how the Moon's appearance changes during a month. The phase may change, but the Moon's "face" stays the same. The same side always points toward us, so we never see the far side.

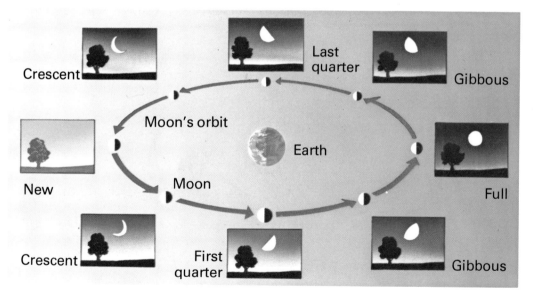

Crescent

Last quarter

Gibbous

Moon's orbit

Earth

New

Moon

Full

Crescent

First quarter

Gibbous

△ The small boxes show what the Moon looks like from Earth at various points in its orbit. The eight views cover a month. When the Moon is "new," its sunlit half faces directly away from Earth, so it is invisible for a few days until a slim crescent gleams in the sky.

9

Eclipses

Sun

The Moon sometimes passes between the Earth and the Sun, cutting off the Sun's light. This is called an eclipse of the Sun.

When the Moon's disc exactly covers that of the Sun, there is a total eclipse. More often only a part of the Sun is covered. This is a partial eclipse. Eclipses do not last very long, as the Moon is speeding through space. Its shadow races across the world at about 1,250 mph (2,000 km/h).

△ The picture above shows how an eclipse of the Sun occurs. The small box shows what a total eclipse looks like from Earth. The black disc is the Moon, exactly covering the Sun. The shining glare is the Sun's corona, its outer layer of gases.

You are lucky if you are in the path of a total eclipse. The shadow path is quite narrow and scientists often travel halfway around the world to see one. Some even fly in jet planes to keep up with the racing shadow.

Sun

The Moon can be eclipsed, too. Sometimes it passes into the Earth's shadow. The Sun's rays are cut off and the Moon dims to a coppery tone until it moves into the sunshine again.

10

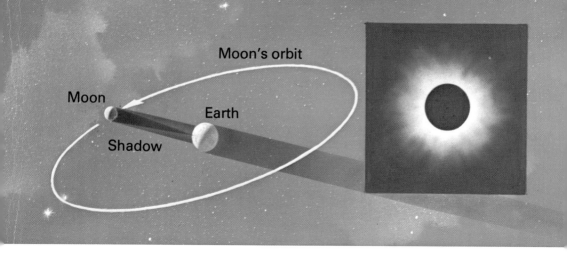

Moon's orbit

Moon

Earth

Shadow

▷ The map plots the paths of solar eclipse shadows across the world for the next few years.

▽ The picture below shows how an eclipse of the Moon occurs. The small box shows what the eclipsed Moon looks like from Earth.

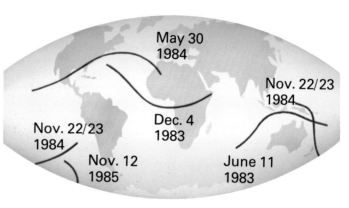

May 30 1984

Nov. 22/23 1984

Nov. 22/23 1984

Dec. 4 1983

Nov. 12 1985

June 11 1983

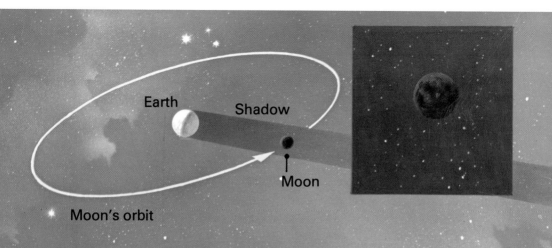

Earth

Shadow

Moon

Moon's orbit

The Moon in close-up

△ This picture, of the crater Copernicus, shows as much detail as you can see through a telescope on Earth. Even so, the central peaks and jagged walls around its edge can be clearly seen. Copernicus is just over 56 miles (90 km) wide.

Astronomers have been studying the Moon through telescopes for hundreds of years. But it was not until space-probes with TV cameras reached the Moon that anyone had a really close look.

In 1959 the Russian craft Luna 1 was the first to pass the Moon. Later that year Luna 3 took blurred pictures of the Moon's hidden far side. This was the first time that anyone had seen it.

In the 1960s both Russia and the USA sent dozens of unmanned craft to the Moon. Some broke down, but the rest took thousands of pictures. By the time astronauts landed there in 1969, American Lunar Orbiter probes had mapped the Moon on both sides. Five Surveyor probes landed on the Moon, taking many close-up pictures.

We now know the geography of the Moon almost as well as we know that of the Earth.

△ Copernicus in
close-up. This picture
was take by the Lunar
Orbiter spaceprobe
shown below. The
mountains reach 12,000
ft (3,700 m) above the
crater floor.

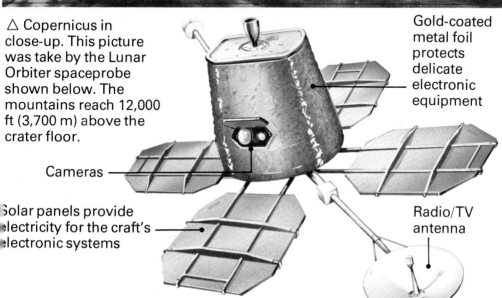

Gold-coated
metal foil
protects
delicate
electronic
equipment

Cameras

Radio/TV
antenna

Solar panels provide
electricity for the craft's
electronic systems

Lunar craters

0   155 miles
        (250 km)

△ Here you can see just how huge some lunar craters are. This map compares Italy with the crater Clavius. It would take nearly three hours to drive across it.

The Moon is pitted with craters of all sizes. They range from a few inches across to vast basins hundreds of miles wide.

Most were formed billions of years ago, soon after the birth of the Moon. A steady hail of cosmic debris crashed on to the surface at up to 45 miles per second (72 km/sec).

Most meteorites were no bigger than grains of sand, but many were huge.

The meteorite that made the crater Clavius must have been over 3 miles (5 km) wide. When it hit the Moon, the explosion was more powerful than the biggest H-bomb. The crater is 146 miles (236 km) wide.

Much of the Moon is covered with dust, stones and rock chips. Meteorites have smashed the surface rocks into tiny fragments. Some parts are very deep in dust and glassy grains.

△ This picture shows
what a big meteor hit
would have looked like.
The fireball of gas, vapor
and shattered rock
fragments is hundreds
of miles wide.

▷ The Moon's far side
has its share of craters,
too. This one was
photographed by the
crew of the Apollo 10
moonship as their craft
swept low over the
surface.

Seas and oceans

The dark areas of the Moon are vast dry plains. Early astronomers thought they were seas and oceans. They are still called by the Latin names "mare" (sea), "oceanus" (ocean) and "sinus" (bay).

The seas and oceans were formed as a result of giant meteorite impacts. The biggest of these were so violent that they cracked the Moon's surface like an eggshell. Molten rock from deep within the Moon bubbled up through the cracks. The lava flooded the bigger craters to form the "seas" and the "oceans."

△ The dark patches are the seas and oceans of the Moon. Oceanus Procellarum, the Ocean of Storms, is marked with an arrow. This is where the astronauts of the Apollo 12 mission landed in 1969. The picture on the right shows them at work.

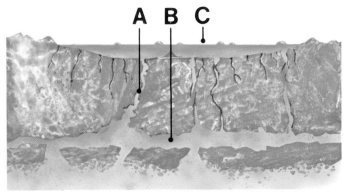

A B C

◁ This picture shows how the lunar seas were made. Meteorites made cracks (A) in the surface. Molten rock (B) under the surface flowed up through the cracks. When the lava cooled and hardened, it formed the fairly smooth "seas" (C).

Mountains and valleys

The mountains of the Moon often reach spectacular heights. Some are almost as high as Mount Everest here on Earth.

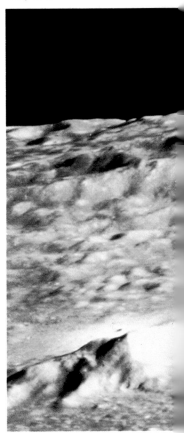

▽ A view of the Moon's far side, desolate almost beyond belief.

The far side of the Moon has even more mountains and craters than the near side. Scientists are not sure why there are so few "seas" there. Perhaps the surface rock layer is thicker and tougher, so underground lava has never been able to force its way to the surface.

Other lunar features include valleys and channels. One of them is called the Hadley Rille. It winds its way for 84 miles (135 km) through the foothills of the Apennine Mountains. It is nearly 1,312 ft (400 m) deep and looks like an old riverbed. It was probably a river, although the liquid was a scorching stream of molten lava, and not water. The Apollo 15 astronauts explored the area when they landed there in 1971.

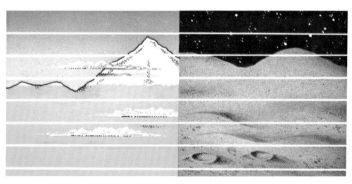

△ The far side of the
Moon. It is covered with
thousands of craters.

△ Mount Everest is the
highest peak on Earth.
Here it is compared with

some lunar peaks, the
Leibnitz Mountains, near
the Moon's South Pole.

Man on the Moon

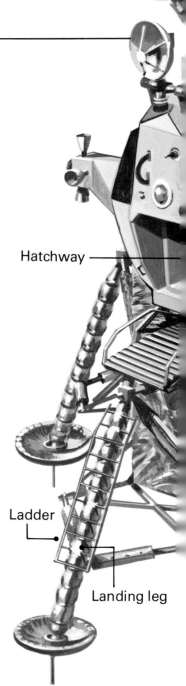

"That's one small step for a man, one giant leap for mankind." With these words, Neil Armstrong became the first man to step on the Moon. It was July 20, 1969, only 12 years after the first Sputnik satellite had been blasted into space by the Russians.

Armstrong and his crewmate, Edwin Aldrin, landed in the *Eagle*, a Lunar Module (LM) like the one shown here. The spidery-looking LM was just a small part of the huge Saturn V rocket used for the Apollo space missions. The complete rocket was 363 ft (111 m) long.

On this first trip, the spacecraft spent only $21\frac{1}{2}$ hours on the Moon. There were five more successful Moon missions. In 1972 the last one, Apollo 17, spent a record-breaking 75 hours on the lunar surface. The astronauts traveled $21\frac{3}{4}$ miles (35 km) and collected many rock samples.

Hatchway

Ladder

Landing leg

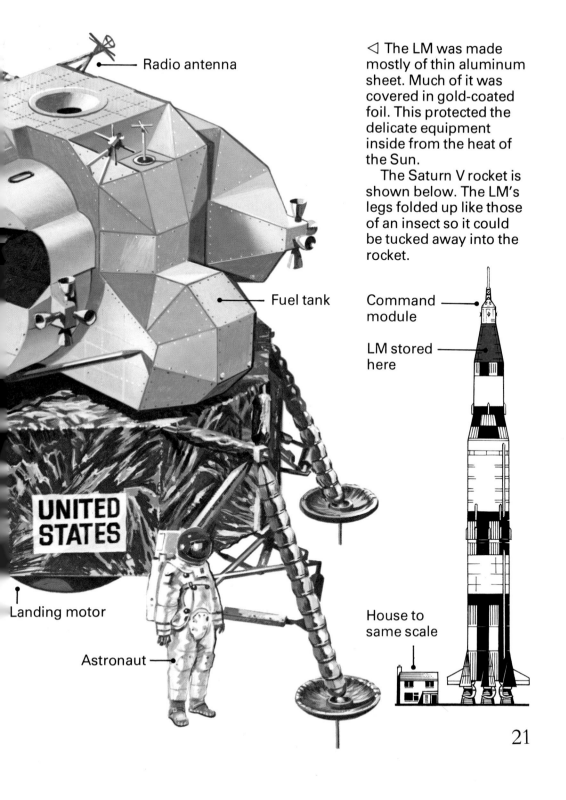

Radio antenna

Fuel tank

UNITED STATES

Landing motor

Astronaut

◁ The LM was made mostly of thin aluminum sheet. Much of it was covered in gold-coated foil. This protected the delicate equipment inside from the heat of the Sun.

The Saturn V rocket is shown below. The LM's legs folded up like those of an insect so it could be tucked away into the rocket.

Command module

LM stored here

House to same scale

21

Lunar explorers

△ Astronaut Harrison Schmitt stands next to a huge boulder high up in the Taurus Littrow mountains. This was the last Moon trip, made by Apollo 17 in 1972.

The last three Apollo missions took a "Lunar Rover" with them. This electric car allowed the astronauts to travel over a wide area at up to $8\frac{1}{2}$ mph (14 km/h). The astronauts had lots of jobs to do. They collected rock samples for scientists back on Earth. All sorts of equipment was set up. One gadget was a seismometer to detect "moon-quakes."

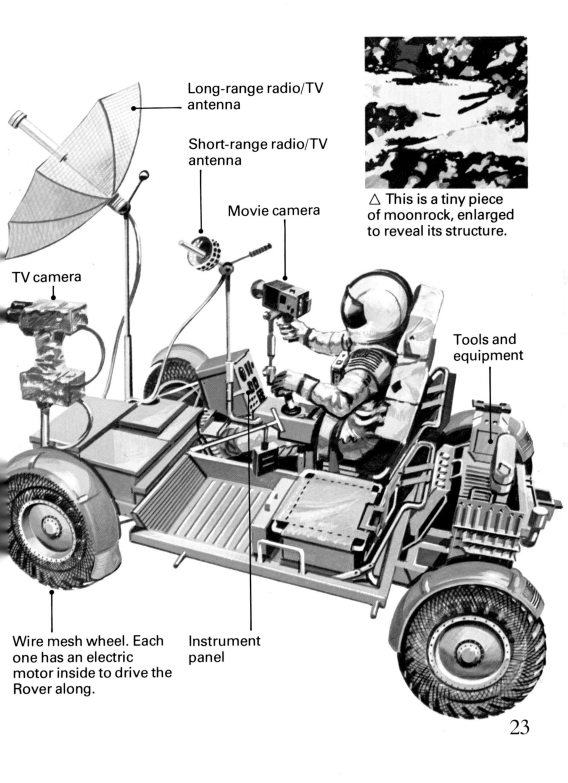

Long-range radio/TV antenna

Short-range radio/TV antenna

Movie camera

△ This is a tiny piece of moonrock, enlarged to reveal its structure.

TV camera

Tools and equipment

Wire mesh wheel. Each one has an electric motor inside to drive the Rover along.

Instrument panel

23

Future Moonbase

Will there be any more trips to the Moon? Many people think it is not worth the money. Others think that there are important scientific experiments still to do. One day it may be worth mining the Moon for its minerals, as its rocks contain useful and valuable metals like aluminum and titanium.

New types of spaceship may make trips to the Moon cheaper. If so, it may be possible to build a Moonbase like the one shown here. Early in the twenty-first century, there may be hundreds of people living and working on the Moon.

It will be a strange way to live. People will have to wear space suits except when in the air-filled domes. There could be a deadly "blow-out" if a dome springs a leak. People may avoid the problem by building underground chambers to live in.

▷ The long lunar night falls over Moonbase One. Two space-suited scientists have just left their Rover to start some experiments.

Behind them, the domes of the base pick up the pearly blue glow from the Earth, hanging low over the horizon.

The base grows its own food in the green plastic tubes. Fresh vegetables grow in them using special liquid instead of soil.

Moon atlas 1

This map shows the upper half of the Moon as we see it from Earth. A pair of binoculars will help you see the smaller features listed.

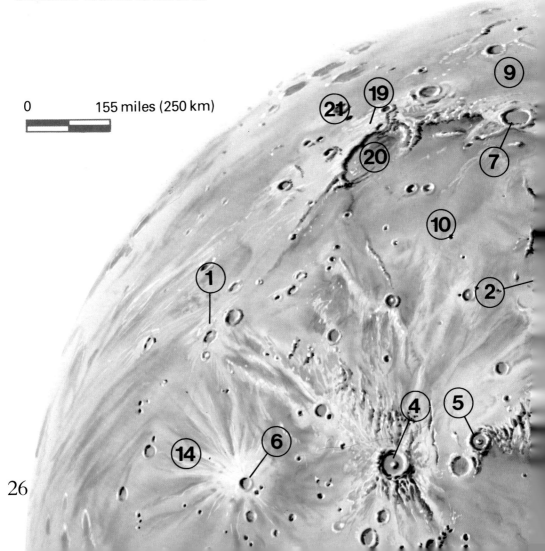

0   155 miles (250 km)

Craters
1 Aristarchus
2 Archimedes
3 Aristoteles
4 Copernicus
5 Eratosthenes
6 Kepler
7 Plato

Maria ("seas")
8 Mare Crisium
   Sea of Crises

9 Mare Frigoris
   Sea of Cold
10 Mare Imbrium
   Sea of Rains
11 Mare Serenitatis
   Sea of Serenity
12 Mare Tranquillitatis
   Sea of Tranquility
13 Mare Vaporum
   Sea of Vapors

Oceanus ("ocean")
14 Oceanus
   Procellarum
   Ocean of Storms

Mountains
15 Apennines
16 Alps
17 Caucasus
18 Haemus
19 Jura

Sini ("bays")
20 Sinus Iridum
   Bay of Rainbows
21 Sinus Roris
   Bay of Dews

Landing sites
22 Apollo 11
23 Apollo 15
24 Apollo 17

27

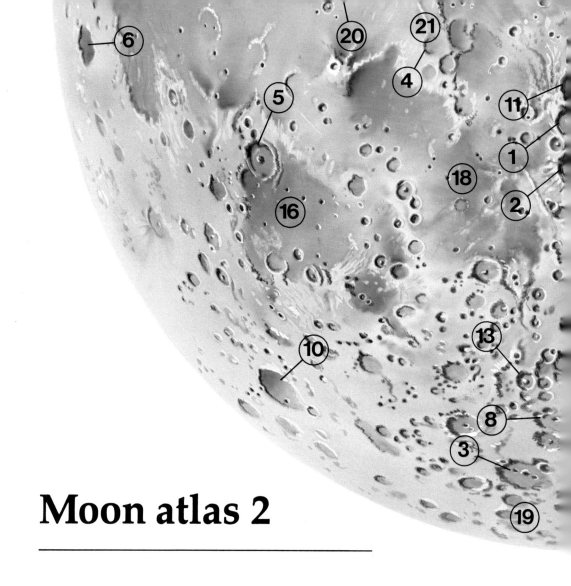

Moon atlas 2

The southern half of the Moon has many large craters. Clavius is one of the biggest, but Tycho shows up more clearly.

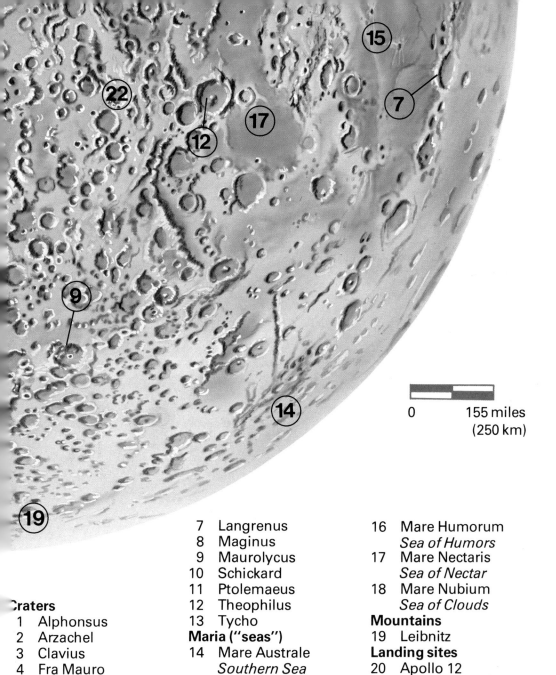

		16	Mare Humorum
7	Langrenus		*Sea of Humors*
8	Maginus	17	Mare Nectaris
9	Maurolycus		*Sea of Nectar*
10	Schickard	18	Mare Nubium
11	Ptolemaeus		*Sea of Clouds*

Craters

		12	Theophilus	**Mountains**	
1	Alphonsus	13	Tycho	19	Leibnitz
2	Arzachel	**Maria ("seas")**		**Landing sites**	
3	Clavius	14	Mare Australe	20	Apollo 12
4	Fra Mauro		*Southern Sea*	21	Apollo 14
5	Gassendi	15	Mare Fecunditatis	22	Apollo 16
6	Grimaldi		*Sea of Fertility*		

29

Glossary

Here is a list of some of the technical words used in the book.

Apollo
The name given to the American Moon-landing program of the 1960s and 1970s. The Saturn rocket which took astronauts to and from the Moon had over two million working parts. A family car has under 3,000.

Crater
Circular depression caused by the impact of a meteorite. Most craters are shallow saucer shapes with central peaks.

Far side
The side of the Moon we cannot see from Earth. The Moon rotates on its axis in exactly the same time it takes to orbit the Earth, so the same face always points toward us.

Gravity
The force of attraction which exists between all objects in the universe. Big objects exert a bigger gravity pull than small ones. The Moon is smaller than the Earth and its gravity is less too, 1/6th that of Earth.

Lunar day
Because the Moon turns so slowly on its axis, its day is much longer than that of the Earth. An Earth day is almost 24 hours long, whereas the Moon's "day" lasts almost a month. Daylight and night-time each last half of this, just under two weeks each.

Lava
Molten rock. Scientists believe that the Moon still has a hot, molten core almost 620 miles (1,000 km) across. By Earthly standards there is little volcanic activity. Most ceased billions of years ago.

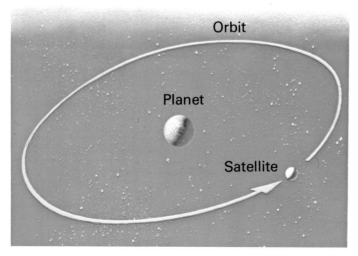

Orbit

Planet

Satellite

Mare
Latin word for sea, (pronounced MAR-ray). Other Latin words used by astronomers include oceanus (oh-shee-AHN-us) for ocean and sinus (SIGH-nuss) for bay.

Meteoroid
Chunk of space rock. Large ones can weigh millions of tons, but most are no bigger than grains of sand. When a meteoroid hits Earth or Moon, it is called a meteorite. Most of the craters of the Moon were made by meteorites. Both Earth and Moon are still sprayed with a constant hail of space "litter." One estimate is that 11,025 tons (10,000 tonnes) of cosmic material fall on the Earth every day.

Orbit
The path in which a small object repeatedly travels around a larger one. The Moon orbits the Earth once a month. The Earth orbits the Sun once a year.

Satellite
Any object which moves

Radio receivers and transmitters

Antenna

Moonquake detection equipment

Solar cells provide electricity

in an orbit around another. The Moon is Earth's natural satellite, but there are thousands of man-made satellites also in orbit.

Seismometer
(size-MOM-uh-ter) Sensitive instrument to detect vibrations in the rocks of Earth or Moon (or any other world!). Seismometers placed on the Moon have detected hundreds of moonquakes – very gentle by Earth standards – and the impact of meteorites. The biggest was a one-ton giant which hit the Moon's far side. The seismometers were very sensitive – they could detect a pea-sized meteorite impact $\frac{1}{2}$ mile (0.8 km) away.

31

Index